BURY
ST EDMUNDS
HISTORY TOUR

First published 2016

Amberley Publishing
The Hill, Stroud,
Gloucestershire, GL5 4EP
www.amberley-books.com

Copyright © Martyn Taylor, 2016
Map contains Ordnance Survey data
© Crown copyright and database right
[2016]

The right of Martyn Taylor to be
identified as the Author of this work
has been asserted in accordance with
the Copyrights, Designs and Patents
Act 1988.

ISBN 978 1 4456 5701 1 (print)
ISBN 978 1 4456 5702 8 (ebook)

British Library Cataloguing in
Publication Data.
A catalogue record for this book is
available from the British Library.

Typesetting by Amberley Publishing.
Printed in Great Britain.

INTRODUCTION

The Saxon homestead Bedricesworth enjoyed royal patronage when King Sigerberht, stepson of the Wuffing King Raedwald of East Anglia, established a *royal ville* here in the early seventh century. Sigerberht had retired from public life to follow a path of piety but answered the call in AD 640 to lead an army against the invading warlord, King Penda of Mercia. Unfortunately, the 'wand' that he waved in battle did not prevent him from being killed. He was later made a saint. This saintly connection was later to lead to another East Anglian king, Edmund, to be laid to rest eventually in the magnificent abbey of St Edmundsbury. Saint Edmund was martyred by the Danes in AD 869. With the coming of the Normans the country was subjugated by the use of castles, but there was no need to build one at Bury St Edmunds as in 1065 there was a French Abbot here, Baldwin. It was he who laid out the town grid still evident today and to commence the building of the huge abbey church in 1080, this continued for over another century to around 1210 despite several calamities. Much of abbey life is detailed in a fascinating chronicle by a monk at the turn of the thirteenth century, Joscelin De Brakelond. The growth of the town relied on the cult of St Edmund, its importance emphasised by the meeting of rebellious barons in 1214 to swear an oath at his shrine to compel King John to agree to Magna Carta. Subsequently parliaments were even held in the town at different times! The town is a member of the Magna Carta Trust, something we are justly very proud of; an 800th anniversary was celebrated here in 2014.

Two events we are not proud of but nevertheless are an indelible part of the history of Bury are the riots that took place in the town. The first in 1327 led to the destruction of the secular entrance to the abbey, that of the Abbeygate, to be rebuilt twenty years later, albeit not in its original position. The second riotous event was in 1381 a year of national unrest known to history as the Peasants Revolt. Two important people then were murdered, the king's Justice and the Prior of the abbey. Both of these incidents may have had something to do with the fact that the all-powerful abbey not only owned and taxed the town but enjoyed the revenues from the eight and half hundreds of the Liberty of St Edmund which was later to become the county of West Suffolk. This munificent gift of the Liberty was given by England's second patron saint, Edward the Confessor, Edmund being the first.

Another royal connection to Bury is that of Queen Mary of France, Henry VIII's younger sister who was buried in the abbey church, 1533. Six years later she was moved to the beautiful parish church of St Marys because of the dissolution of our Benediction abbey, 1539 – over 500 years of abbey rule brought to an end. The Guildhall Feoffees, a medieval charity still in existence today, were to run the town until 1606 when Bury received its first charter. Two years later a disastrous fire engulfed the town centre, which is why most of the oldest properties in the town are on the southern side. Today their timber frames are hidden from view as they suffered from 'Georgianisation' – brick facades hiding their ancient past.

Over centuries the wealth of the town grew on the backs of sheep. The wool trade helped to generate wealth for local gentry such as the Drurys of Hawstead, Herveys of Ickworth, Davers of Rushbrooke and the Oakes family. The genteel appreciation of our town was described by one visitor to the town as 'The Montpellier of England'. With the coming of the Victorian age, industrialisation was slow to have any impact on the town, but the Greene King Brewery and Bobys Engineering were at the forefront of employment. For those unfortunate enough to be unemployed there were two workhouses to keep the indolent busy. 1914 saw the creation of the Diocese of St Edmundsbury and Ipswich; we have the cathedral, Ipswich the seat of the Bishop. In 2005, thanks to a Heritage Lottery Grant and the generosity of a bequest by Stephen Dykes-Bower, the late architect for the Diocese, it was completed, the last cathedral to be finished in the country. The people who come to Bury St Edmunds, whether as tourists, for work or to visit relatives, are surprised at what a wonderful town it is. A survey in recent years listed our town as one of the top ten places in the country to live. With an eclectic mix of shops and a wealth of heritage, you don't need to have a love of history to appreciate its uniqueness.

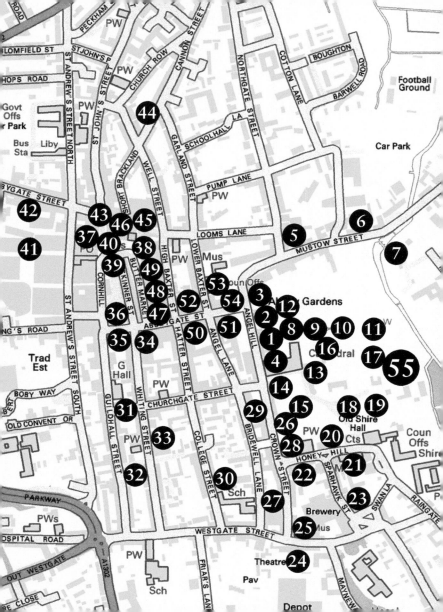

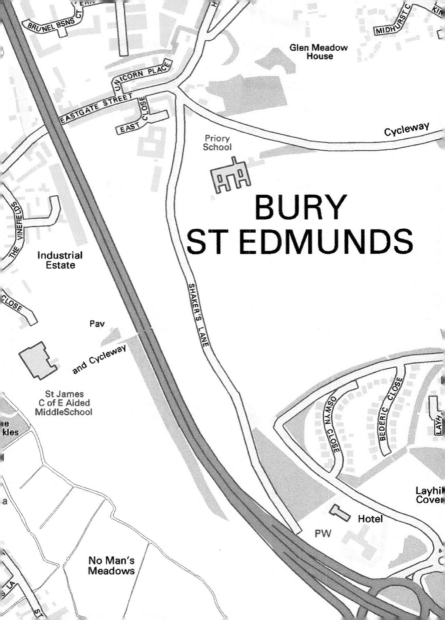

BURY
ST EDMUNDS

BRUNEL BSNS CT

MIDHURST C

Glen Meadow
House

UNICORN PLACE

EASTGATE STREET

EAST CLOSE

Cycleway

Priory
School

THE VINEFIELDS

Industrial
Estate

CLOSE

Pav

and Cycleway

SHAKER'S LANE

St James
C of E Aided
MiddleSchool

kles

OSWYN CLOSE

BEDERIC CLOSE

LAYH

Layhil
Cover

a

Hotel

PW

No Man's
Meadows

ST LA

1. ANGEL HILL, ANGEL HOTEL

The Virginia-creeper-covered Angel Hotel, built 1775 on the site of three inns, dominates this open area. Charles Dickens stayed here, including the Angel in his first novel, *The Pickwick Papers*. A blue plaque testifies this. The important Bury Fair was held here from early medieval times until 1871, abolished by Parliament for being a nuisance. A popular annual Christmas Fayre rivalling its ancient forebear is now a major attraction. The 'Pillar of Salt' is a listed traffic sign from 1935.

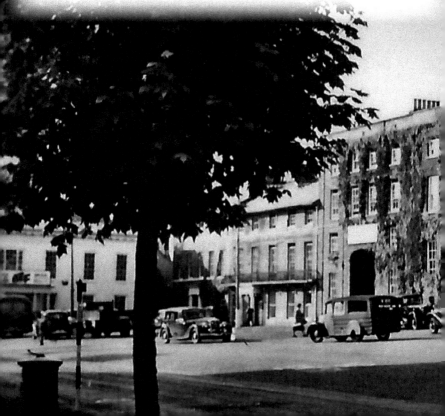

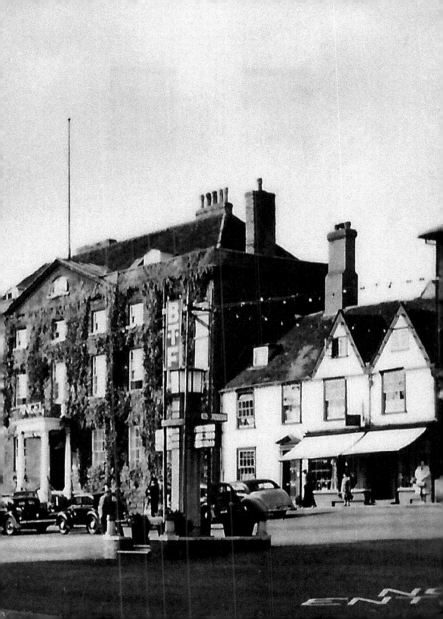

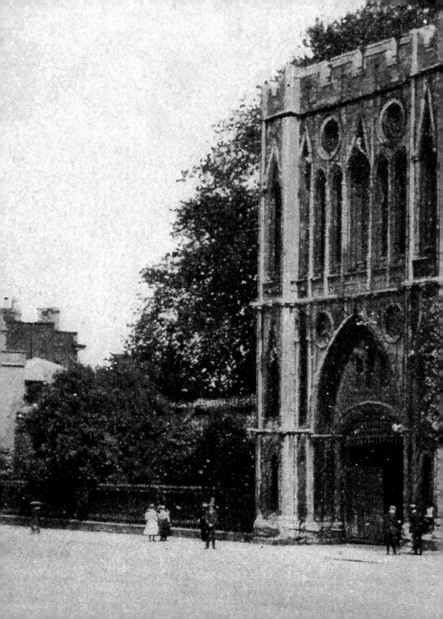

2. ANGEL HILL, ABBEYGATE

In 1327 the townspeople revolted against the oppressive control of the abbey, destroying the abbey's secular entrance. In those days the gate stood opposite Abbeygate Street, known then as The Cook Row. By 1347 this very iconic gateway was finished in the English decorated style with niches for statues and embellishments. At 60 feet high, and with walls up to 6 feet thick, a small garrison was stationed here by leave of the king. The portcullis, a Victorian replacement, has never been lowered.

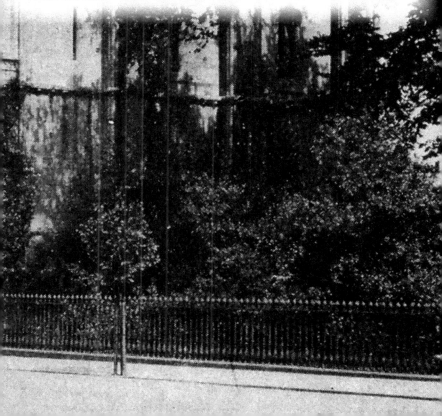

3. ANGEL HILL, FORMER BOROUGH OFFICES

Sybil Andrews, famous local artist, created the heraldic cartouche on the 1937 pediment with the Borough motto in Latin, 'shrine of a king, cradle of the law', for the Borough Arts & Craft architect Basil Oliver. The rear 1966 borough office extension has now been converted to apartments. The house to the left was once owned by eighteenth-century philanthropist Dr Poley Clopton; he left a bequest to build an asylum (rest home) in the churchyard, now the deanery.

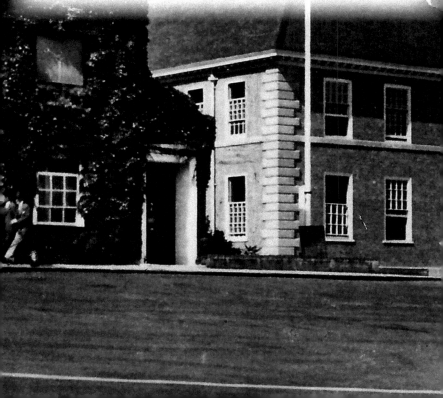

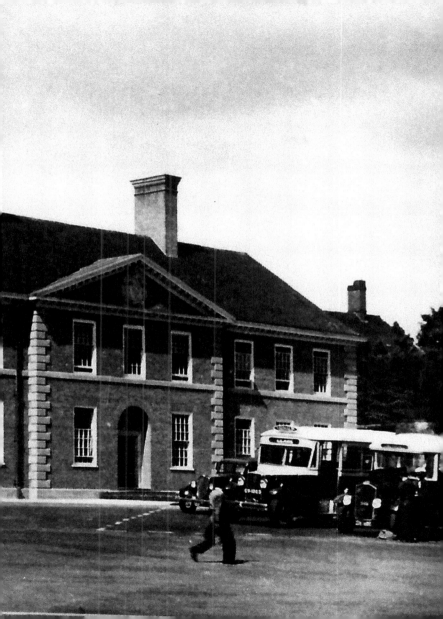

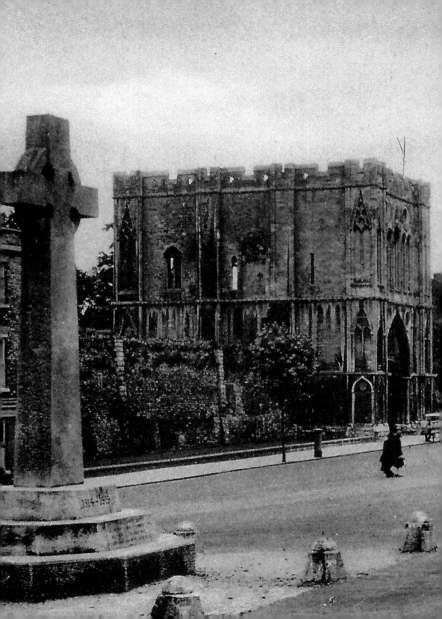

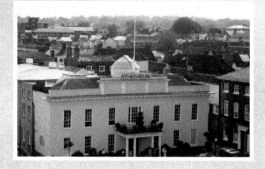

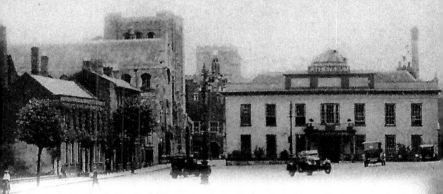

4. ANGEL HILL, THE ATHENAEUM

In 1801 local banker James Oakes purchased this building at the southern end of Angel Hill. Francis Sandys, the architect of Ickworth Mansion, is thought to have carried out the refurbishment work. Oakes then sold off shares in the property to some fellow members of the thirty-seven-man corporation, hence Subscription Rooms. Over the years its Adam-style ballroom has played host to many important functions and has an observatory installed after a lecture in 1859 by Sir George Airey, Astronomer Royal.

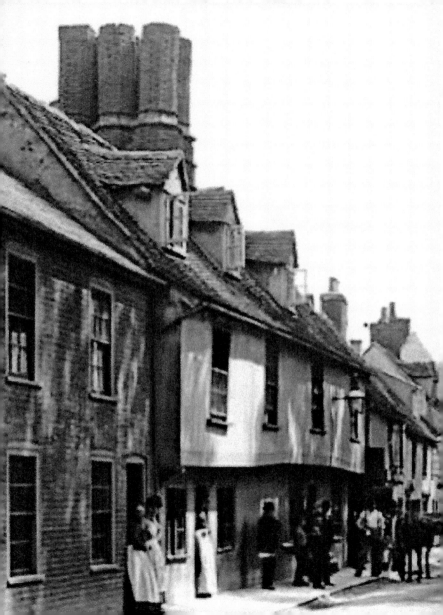

5. MUSTOW STREET

Angel Hill used to be known as le Mustowe, The Muster, a place to gather. This name was carried down into this narrow street at the side of the abbey's precinct north wall. In 1926, despite much opposition, it was agreed to widen the road. The old timber-frame cottages including the 200-year-old Star Inn (closed in 1923) were demolished. One small concession to the past was the reuse of ancient timbers in the rebuild of No. 17, Mustow Street.

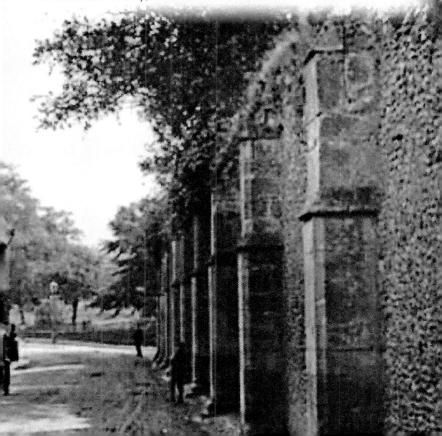

6. EASTGATE STREET, THE FOX

Possibly the oldest public house in the town, it escaped the ravages of the great fire of Bury in 1608 which started further up Eastgate Street in a malsters. Inside, the roof has many fine timbers including an octagonal crown post. The Victorian exterior makeover of pseudo-Jacobean, black-varnished timbers was removed by Greene King in 1922, as were several layers of paint on genuine Jacobean panelling internally. Once a drover's inn, it is now an open-plan gastro-pub.

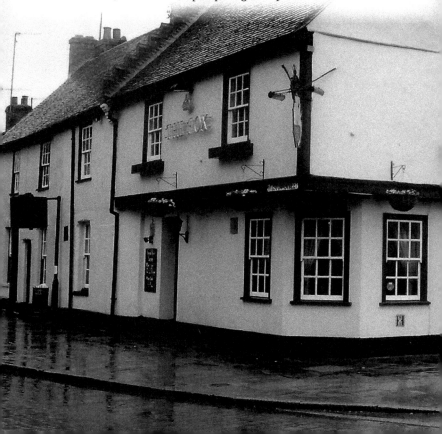

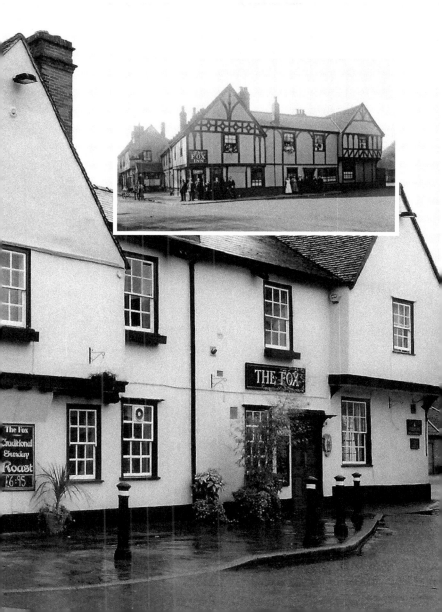

7. EASTGATE STREET, ABBOTS BRIDGE

Spanning the River Lark, this very iconic bridge has open buttresses on one side through which planks could run; this allowed the townspeople to cross the river. On the abbey side, the monks could cross uninhibited, an iron grating being lowered if necessary to prevent any unwanted visitors on the river. The Eastgate, the only town gate controlled by the abbot, was also nearby – handy in times of trouble. The bridge has changed very little in nearly 900 years.

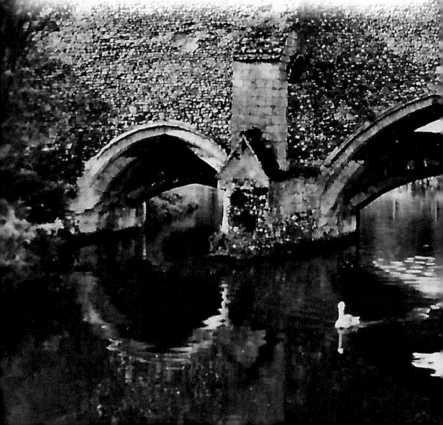

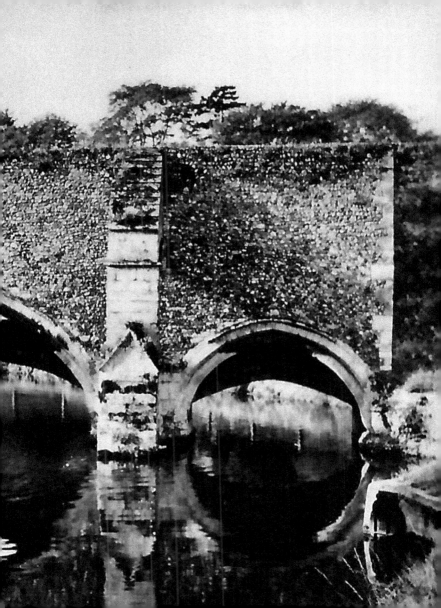

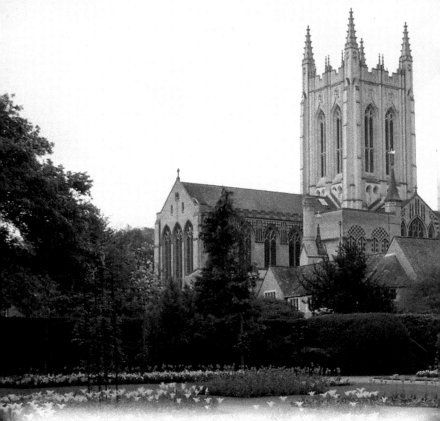

8. CATHEDRAL FROM ABBEY GARDENS

When the architect of St Edmundsbury and Ipswich Diocese, the acrophobic Stephen Dykes Bower, died in 1994, he left over £2 million in his will for the addition of a tower. He had already completed major works here including a new choir and crossing. Former associate Hugh Mathew was able to finish the work when a successful bid to the Millennium Commission enabled the tower to start in 2000. It was finished in 2005 to triumphant acclaim.

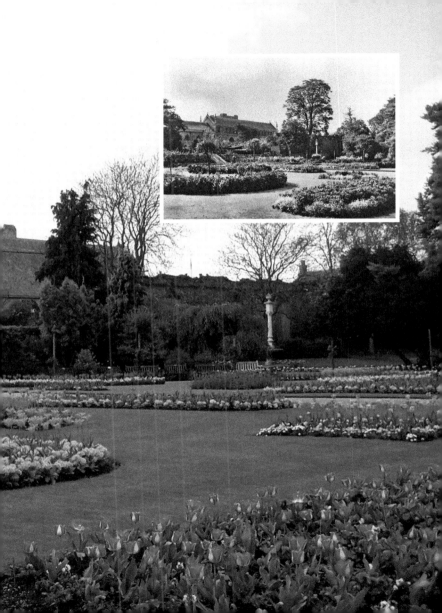

9. ABBEY GARDENS, FOUNTAIN

This ornamental drinking fountain stood in the Traverse after the Marquess of Bristol gave it to the town in 1871. It was moved to the Abbey Gardens in 1939 to create space for traffic and was used as a planter. Recently the sundial and inscription on the face of the Portland stone has been found to be of major importance in the world of horology. Calculations on a graph called 'the equation of time' relates to Greenwich Mean Time.

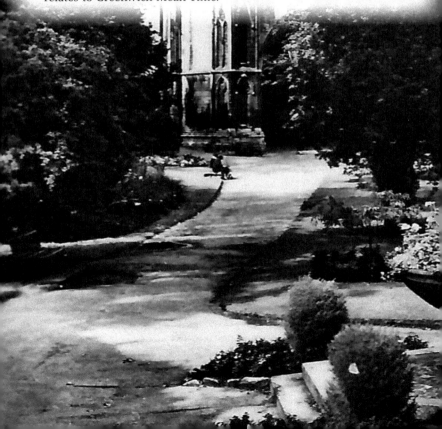

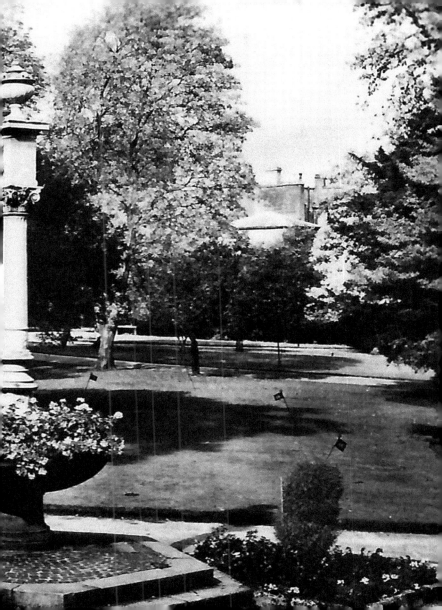

10. ABBEY GARDENS, MAGNA CARTA PLAQUES

Just visible among the 1909 undergrowth are two plaques on a column of the abbey church's crossing. Both plaques were put there in the mid-nineteenth century under the auspices of Dr Donaldson, the headmaster of Bury Grammar School. They tell the story of Magna Carta with a list of the barons who met here in 1214. 2014 saw the 800-year anniversary here; Bury St Edmunds is one of the five members of the Magna Carta Trust.

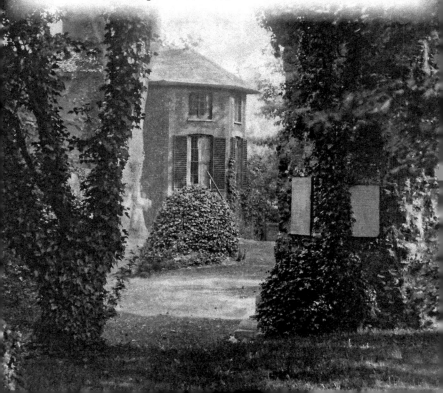

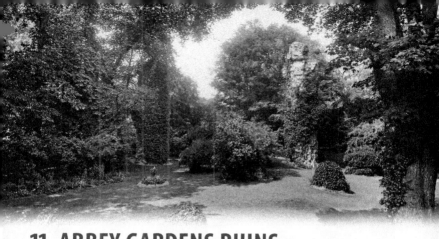

11. ABBEY GARDENS RUINS

Buria Sancti Edmundi owes its very existence to the interred remains here of the former king of East Anglia. St Edmundsbury Abbey was once one of the greatest in the country, on a site of several acres. The construction of the abbey's buildings consisted of limestone blocks with a flint and lime mortar core. All that is left now is a mere glimpse of its magnificent abbey church, dissolved in 1539 by Henry VIII. The ruins were overgrown until clearance in the late 1950s.

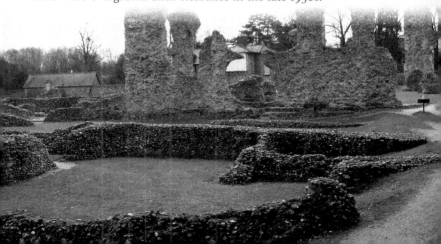

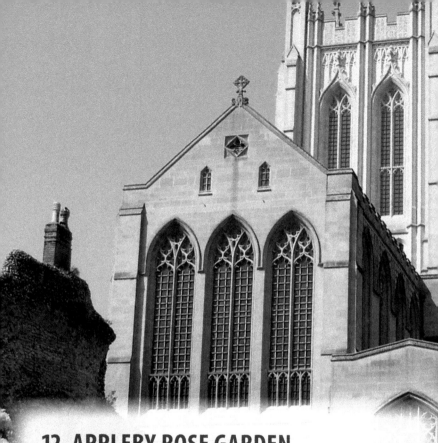

12. APPLEBY ROSE GARDEN

John Tate Appleby was an American serviceman sent over to England in 1945 to teach celestial navigation to American flyers; he was not required as they were flying by day then. The highly educated Appleby so enjoyed his sojourn that he wrote a book called *A Suffolk Summer*, which is still in print today. The royalties were left by him to help create and maintain this wonderful garden. There are various memorials to servicemen here. Today it is a place of tranquillity and contemplation.

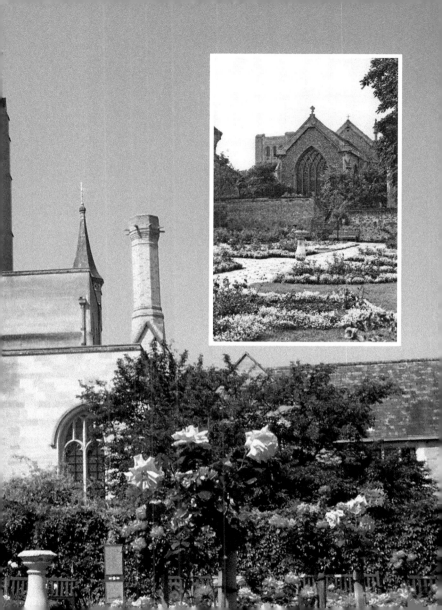

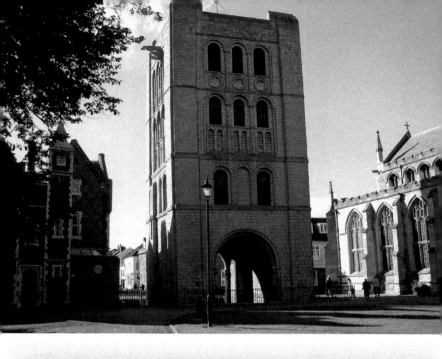

13. GREAT CHURCHYARD, THE NORMAN TOWER

Abbot Anselm, abbacy 1120–48, built this impressive 80-foot-high gateway to the abbey church. Constructed from Barnack limestone, it is one of the finest Norman buildings in the country. However in danger of collapse some 700 years later, restoration was undertaken, which included removing properties abutting the tower. Adjacent Savings Bank, a pseudo-Jacobean house, was built at the same time to designs by tower restoration and Gothic Revival architect Lewis Cottingham. The tower is now the belfry for the cathedral.

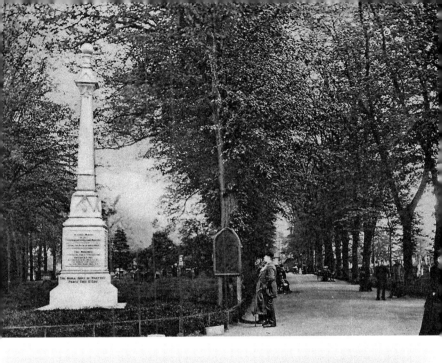

14. GREAT CHURCHYARD, THE MARTYRS MEMORIAL

This Purbeck limestone obelisk was erected by public subscription in 1903 by local stonemasons, Hanchets. Recorded on it are the details of seventeen Protestant martyrs who perished during the reign of 'Bloody' Mary, 1553–58. Strangely none of the victims were from Bury but from such places as Hadleigh, Coddenham and Stoke by Nayland. They were ordinary folk, such as weavers and labourers. It holds a prominent place in the churchyard, a fitting reminder to those brave souls.

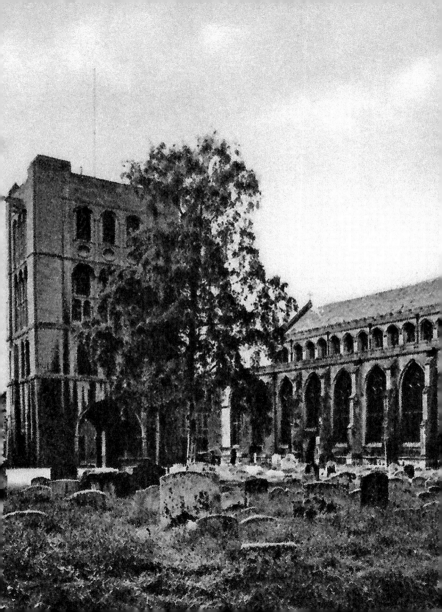

15. GRAVESTONES BY CATHEDRAL

This part of the churchyard by St James near the abbey's west front was covered in graves up until the late 1950s, after which the headstones were removed and the graves' occupants left in situ. The cathedral then still had its Victorian chancel and no tower. A sward of grass was laid, then a remarkable bronze statue of St Edmund, created by renowned sculptress Dame Elizabeth Frink, was erected in 1976 to observe the amalgamation of East and West Suffolk in 1974 – the county of Suffolk.

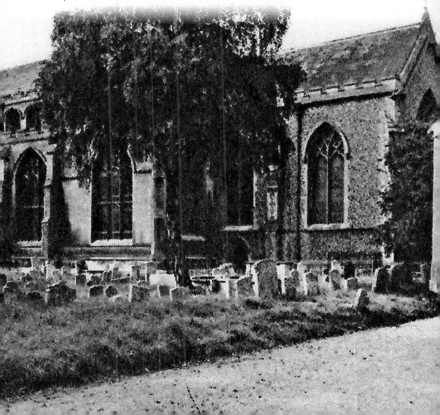

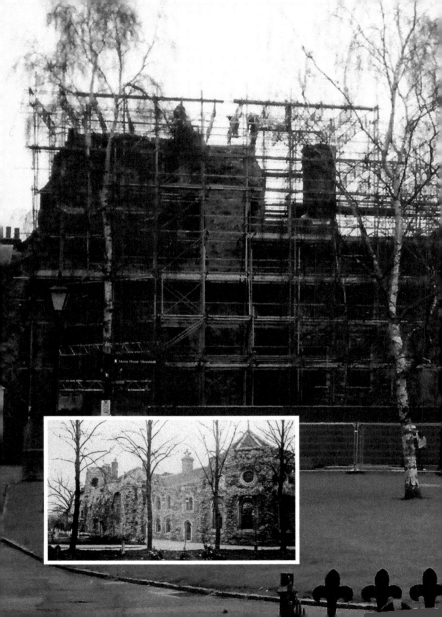

16. THE WEST FRONT OF THE ABBEY CHURCH

At 246 feet across, it was one of the widest in the country. With octagonal chapels and a tower which we can only speculate the height of, this must have presented a magnificent entrance to the abbey church. The last great procession to go through its central arch was that of the funeral cortege of French queen Mary Tudor, Henry VIII's sister, in 1533. After the Dissolution, houses were built into the ruined front, thankfully restored in recent years.

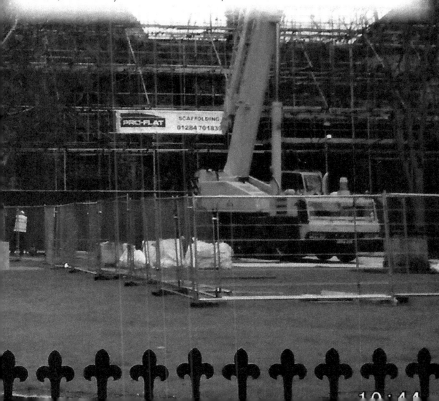

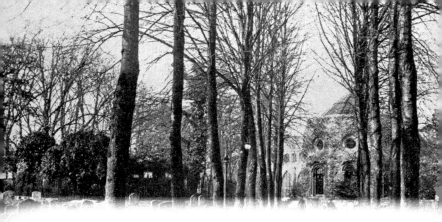

17. GREAT CHURCHYARD AVENUE

This is one of two lime tree avenues in the Great Churchyard. On the right is Samson's Tower, part of the west front of the abbey church; it became the Probate Office in later years. On the left is the ivy-covered ruined charnel house from 1301. In 1721 a barbarous attack in the churchyard by Arundel Coke on his brother-in-law left him disfigured, resulting in Coke paying the full penalty! Thankfully all now is tranquil.

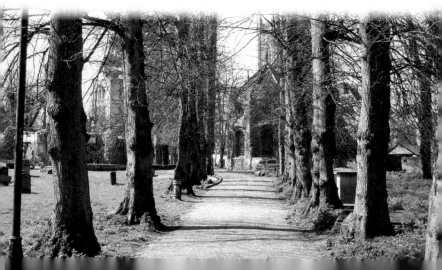

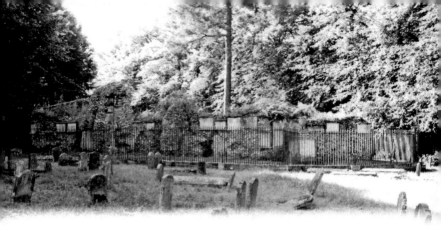

18. GREAT CHURCHYARD, CHARNEL HOUSE

This consecrated bone depository was founded in 1301 by Abbot John De Northwold amid concerns of the treatment of bones found in disused graves. After the Dissolution it was used for many purposes including a blacksmiths' forge. Around the outside are various plaques to, among others, Victorian novelist Henry Cockton, Bartholomew Gosnold, founder of Jamestown, and Sarah Lloyd, hanged for burglary – her sombre epitaph issues a warning unto thousands. In 1845 some poor soul fell through into the bone-strewn crypt.

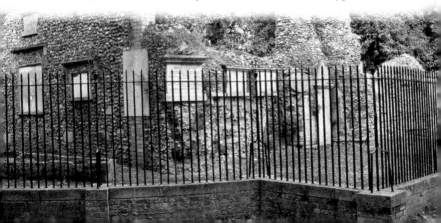

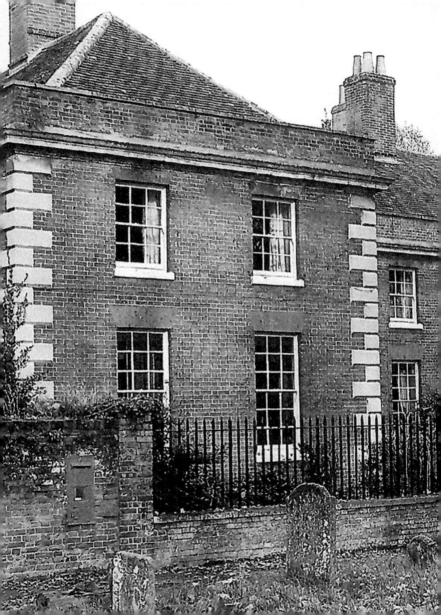

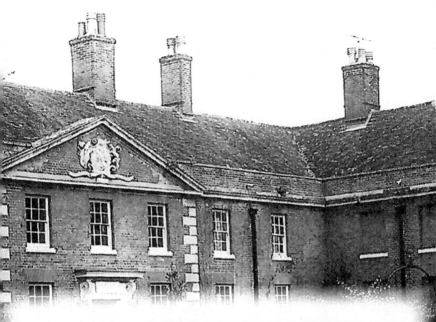

19. GREAT CHURCHYARD, CLOPTON'S ASYLUM

This fine Georgian property was built out of the generosity of Dr Poley Clopton, who by his will of 1730 left provision for a retirement home for three widows and three widowers from St James's and St Mary's parishes providing they were aged over sixty and had not been a burden on their respective parishes; they were to have a manservant and housekeeper to look after them. In old French above the doorway it says 'henceforth it must not be forgotten'. It is now the deanery.

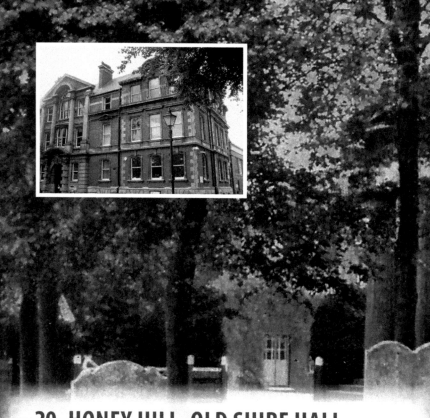

20. HONEY HILL, OLD SHIRE HALL

This rather grand-looking edifice was built in 1841 with pediment and columns. You would have thought it would stand for many years; however it was demolished to make way for the current building of 1906/07 by local architect Archie Ainsworth Hunt. In use now as a magistrates' court, the future of this important service is now at risk as sweeping cuts to the judiciary are to be implemented, meaning Bury will lose a connection it is proud of – 'Cradle of the Law'.

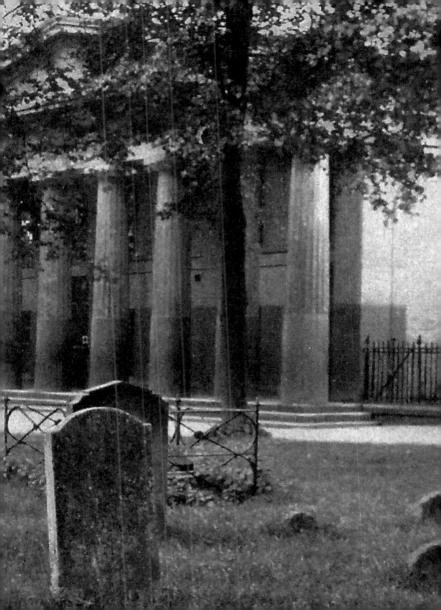

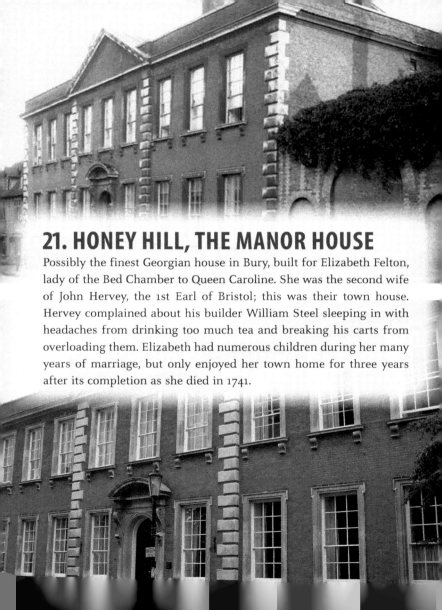

21. HONEY HILL, THE MANOR HOUSE

Possibly the finest Georgian house in Bury, built for Elizabeth Felton, lady of the Bed Chamber to Queen Caroline. She was the second wife of John Hervey, the 1st Earl of Bristol; this was their town house. Hervey complained about his builder William Steel sleeping in with headaches from drinking too much tea and breaking his carts from overloading them. Elizabeth had numerous children during her many years of marriage, but only enjoyed her town home for three years after its completion as she died in 1741.

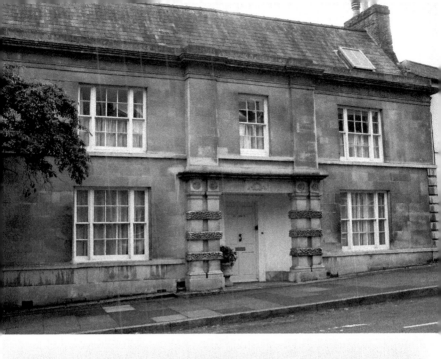

22. HONEY HILL, ST DENYS

On this fifteenth-century timber-framed house, a stone façade – one of only two in the town – was put on by stonemason Thomas Singleton. He was responsible for the fine carvings on the Market Cross. A previous occupier was barrister Arundel Coke who in 1721 tried to kill his brother-in-law in a vicious plot to get his fortune after unsuccessfully investing in the national scandal known as 'The South Seas Bubble'.

23. ST MARY'S SQUARE

It was known in Saxon times as The Horse Market and is today a very desirable place to live, the fine houses surrounding the magnificent planter of Mark Blanchard from 1874. Made from frost-free terracotta, it has been restored in recent years. A former Methodist chapel from 1811 is now a private house, and at No. 6 from 1806–15 lived Thomas Clarkson, the promoter of the emancipation bill that freed slaves in 1833.

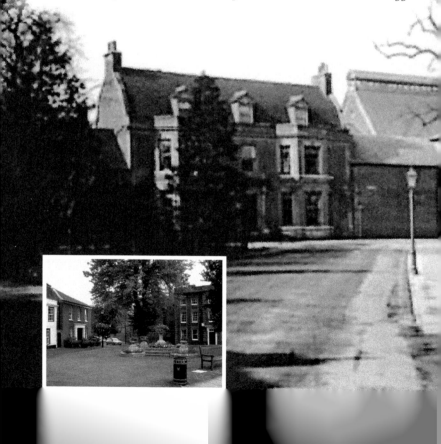

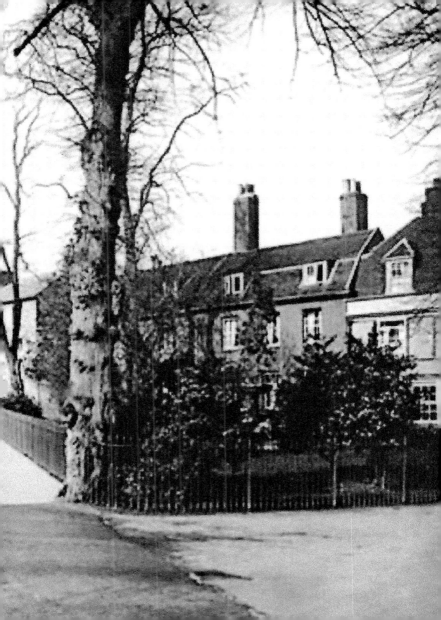

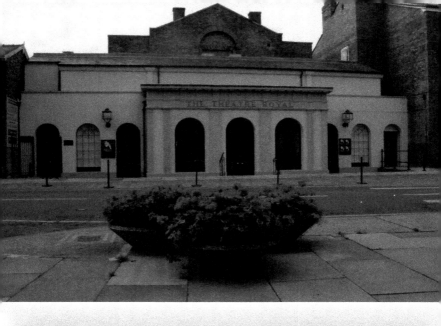

24. WESTGATE STREET, THEATRE ROYAL

William Wilkins, 1778–1839 chose this site for the 'New Theatre' in Westgate Street because of its natural sloping gradient. It opened in 1819 and perhaps its most famous performance was the 1892 inaugural production of *Charlie's Aunt*. The theatre closed in 1925, languishing as a Greene King barrel store until in 1959 being rescued by concerned theatre-lovers. It reopened in 1965 and is now run by the National Trust as the only working Regency theatre in the country with a varied programme, its pantomimes proving to be very popular.

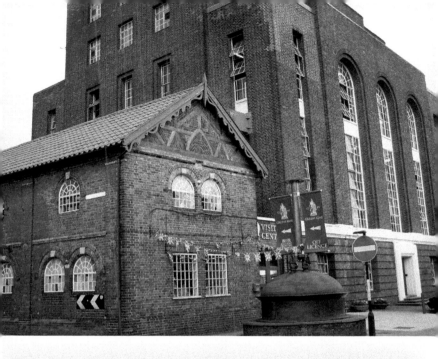

25. WESTGATE STREET, GREENE KING BREWERY

Greene King was formed in 1887 with the amalgamation of Fred King's St Edmunds Brewery and Edward Greene's Westgate Brewery. The large brewhouse was opened in January 1939 after having several setbacks. The visitor's centre as the electrician's workshop suffered a disastrous fire in 1979 just as work on the roof was nearing completion. The brewery tours are very popular nowadays and GK are one of the largest independent breweries in the country.

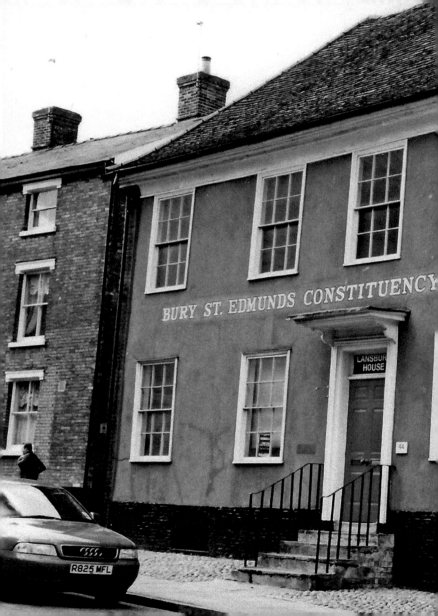

26. CROWN STREET, LANSBURY HOUSE

Until its closure in 1903, this was The Three Tuns, one of only two public houses in Crown Street. It was later to become the headquarters of the local Labour Party, Lansbury House, from 1949 to 1997. George Lansbury was chairman of the national Labour Party during the 1930s. Always painted in the parties bright red hues, since it became a private house the colours are more subdued. Adjacent, Tuns Lane is a reminder of the past connection to the property.

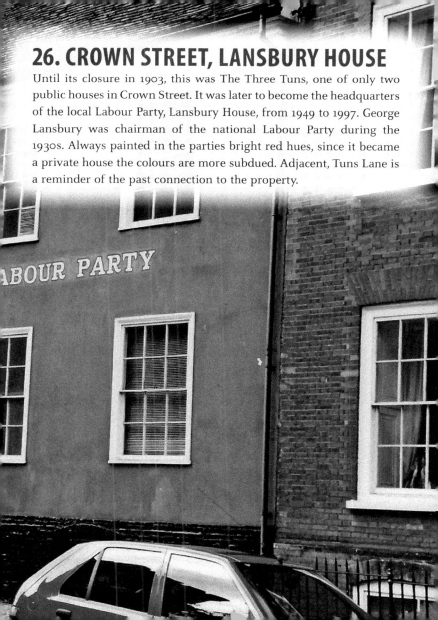

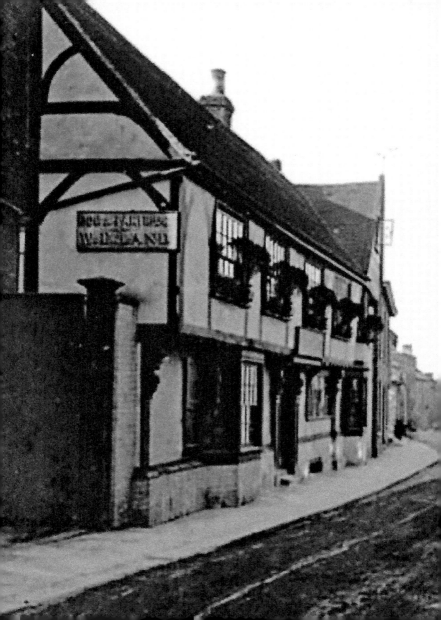

27. CROWN STREET, DOG & PARTRIDGE

Once the Mermaid Inn, this ancient pub in Crown Street was taken over by Greene King in 1872. Landlords applied for midnight extensions whenever a popular performance at the nearby Theatre Royal took place. The theatre's patrons no doubt enjoyed the rook pies, a specialty of the pub, the rooks being shot in the churchyard at nearby St Mary's. Throughout the years many alterations have taken place, internally and externally, including removal of mock-Jacobean timbers and contentious changes of inn signs.

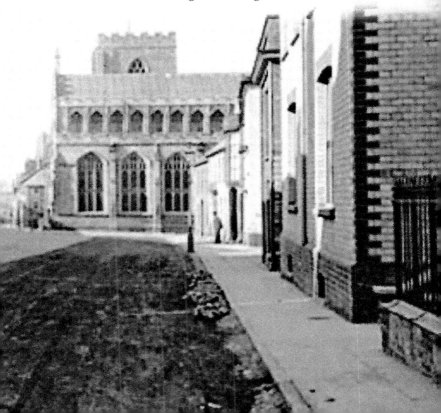

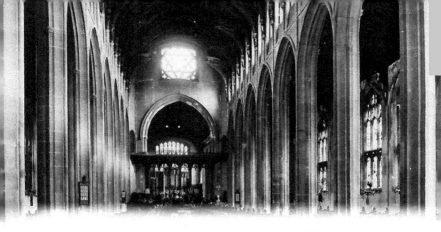

28. CROWN STREET, ST MARY'S INTERIOR

As you look down the nave of St Mary's you appreciate the beauty of this, one of the largest parish churches in England. In this picture, the church is about to celebrate a harvest festival service. The oldest endowed service in the country, from 1481 to benefactor Jankyn Smyth, is still celebrated here in June. The magnificent hammer-beam roof is of a procession of angels leading to the East Window of 1844 with the martyrdom of St Edmund in stained glass.

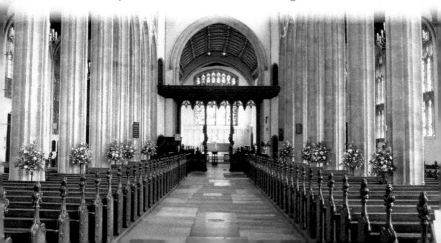

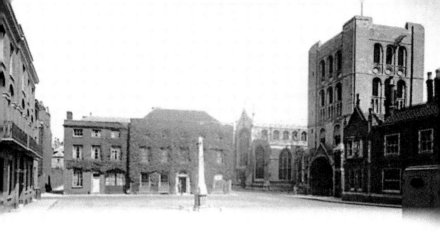

29. CHEQUER SQUARE

This was an important open space in front of the religious entrance to the abbey. Fifteenth-century wealthy merchant John Baret's house, a forces study centre in the Second World War, is on the left, almost facing Norman Tower House, once the Savings Bank. At the northern side of the Square is St Edmunds Masonic Lodge, closed recently but originated from 1890 when the Six Bells, an important former coaching inn, finished. The obelisk, moved in 1977 to create more parking, has the borough coat of arms on, almost obliterated.

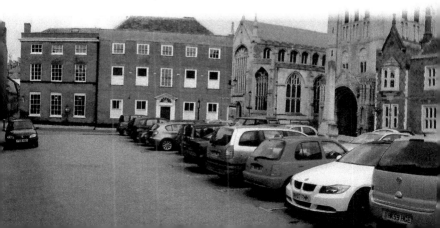

30. COLLEGE STREET, GUILDHALL FEOFFMENT SCHOOL

The Commercial School in College Street was established, as was its elementary counterpart in Bridewell Lane, by the Guildhall Feoffees, (founded in medieval times by Jankyn Smyth). As the Commercial School it was to teach 158 boys not only the three R's but also French, Latin, surveying etc. in preparation for professional careers. Henry Kendall designed the school in 1843. Both schools amalgamated in 1931, and is now somewhat enlarged since then. The stepped parapet with the armorial shields have now gone.

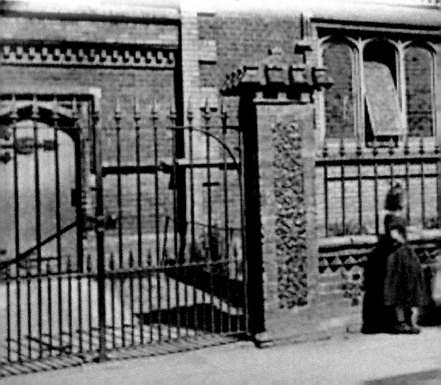

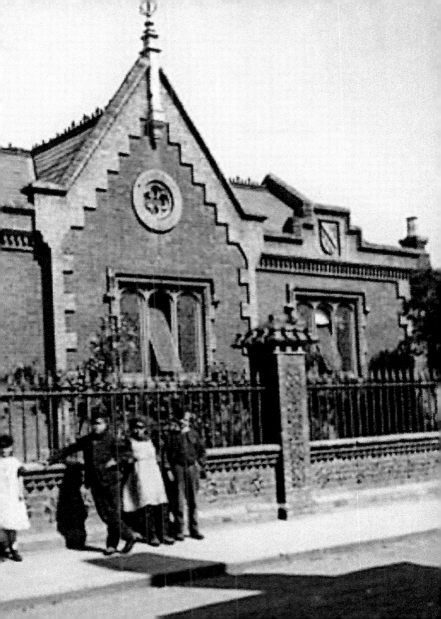

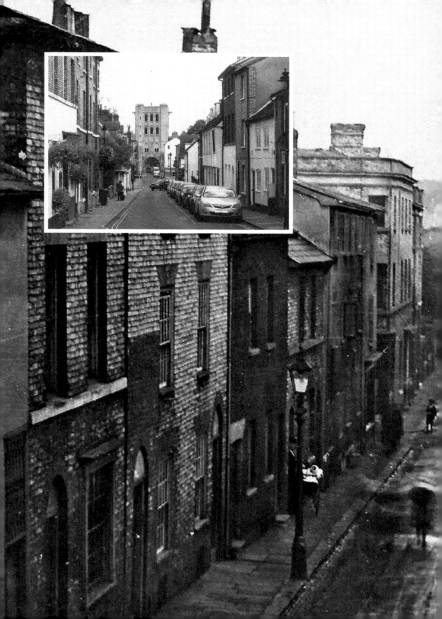

31. CHURCHGATE STREET

A brooding image of one of the main streets of the historic core of the town, making Bury the oldest purposely laid out town in the country. This street was once a processional way through The Norman Tower, a religious gateway to the abbey. On the left is the Unitarian Meeting House. Multifunctional now, it started its life as a Presbyterian chapel in 1711. It is architecturally beautiful, both externally and internally, with a wonderful pulpit and original box pews.

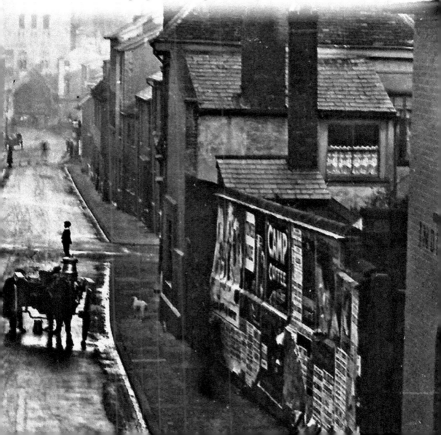

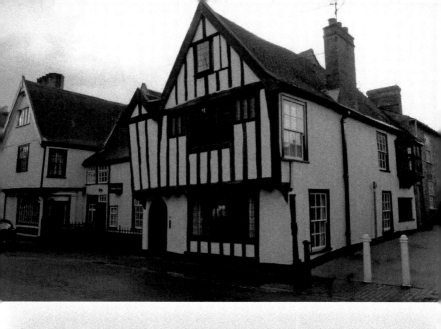

32. WHITING STREET, NOS 61–63

Once a hall house from the fifteenth century, these three houses would not look out of place in Lavenham. It was originally a rich merchant's house, someone who could afford to flaunt these quality timbers, while No. 61 has a really old shop window, its glass bending and bowing. On the side of No. 63 is an oriel window with a carving of an angel, thought to have come from a church in the area.

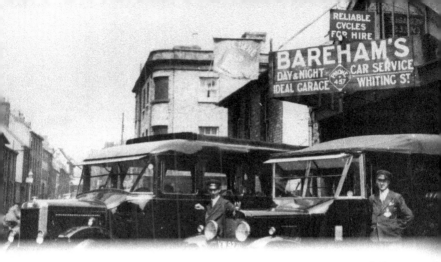

33. WHITING STREET, ROGERS' GARAGE

Barehams offered a full taxi service from their 'Ideal Garage'. Later Fairtax Travel of Brentgovel Street also had a garage here. Brothers Pat and Neville Rogers started theirs in 1979; Pat's ramp on the right, Neville's the left. In 1997 it was the last town-centre garage to dispense fuel. Sadly after Neville died, the garage closed in 2010. Patrick House on the right and Neville House on the left are the new houses, a nice touch by the developers.

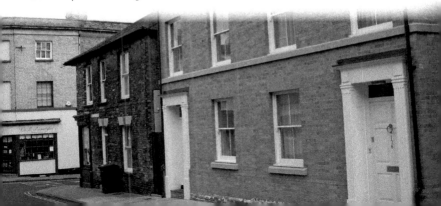

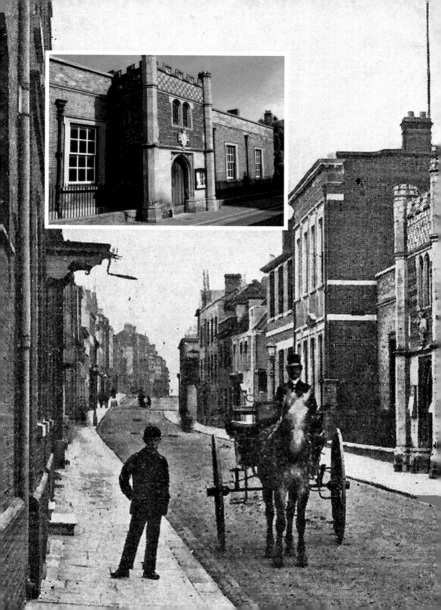

34. GUILDHALL STREET

A much used street scene of the Guildhall, possibly the oldest civic building in the country. Recent evidence uncovered details how it has been serving the people of Bury St Edmunds from around the twelfth century, as a meeting hall, court and council chamber. During the Second World War the Royal Observer Corps had an Ops room inside, still here; perhaps it is the only one of its kind in the country? The Guildhall Project is planning to create a heritage centre here.

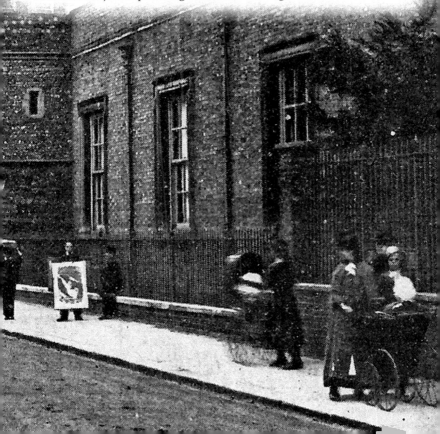

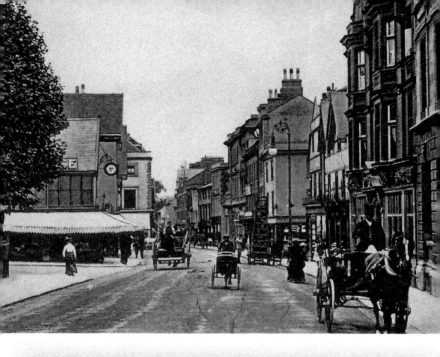

35. ABBEYGATE STREET AND CORN EXCHANGE

One of Bury's major public buildings was built by Lot Jackaman in 1861/62. Mid-twentieth-century wrestling and roller-skating were held here. It was saved from demolition in 1959/60 and in 1970 it was split in two – shops below, public hall above. Note the railings that once enclosed it. J D Wetherspoons controversially leased the public venue, The Corn Exchange pub opening 5 June 2012. Opposite were the Alliance Assurance offices, now the Café Rouge restaurant.

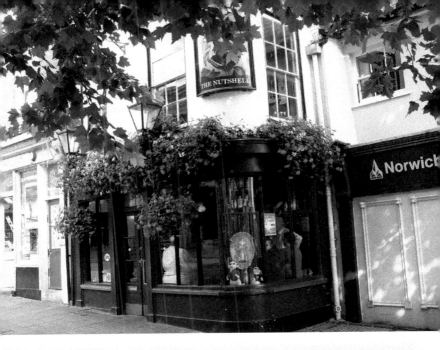

36. TRAVERSE, THE NUTSHELL

Forget any contrived suitors, this IS the smallest pub in Britain: the bar is 15 feet × 7 feet and the record number of people to get inside this diminutive hostelry is 102 – don't forget a dog as well! It started life as a beerhouse in 1873 and has acquired, over the years, bank notes stuck to the ceiling, a mummified cat and other curios. A visit to the town is isn't complete without having a small libation here!

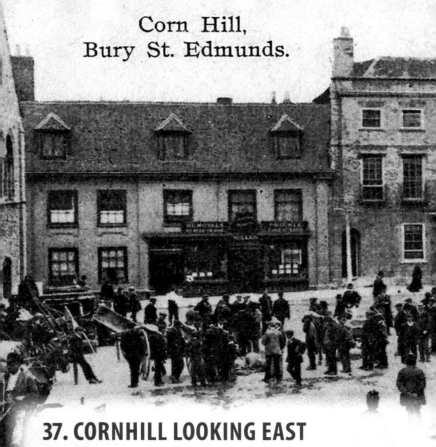

Corn Hill,
Bury St. Edmunds.

37. CORNHILL LOOKING EAST

From medieval times, this part of the Beast Market was also known as Hogs Hill. The great fire of Bury in 1608 swept through the town centre, reducing it to ashes except for the twelfth-century Moyses Hall on the left. In 1828 the Beast Market moved to St Andrews Street South. Starbucks, No. 20, is where the Bullen family had their cabinet-making and removals premises from 1855 until the 1920s. Marks & Spencer's original façade is only one of a handful left in the country.

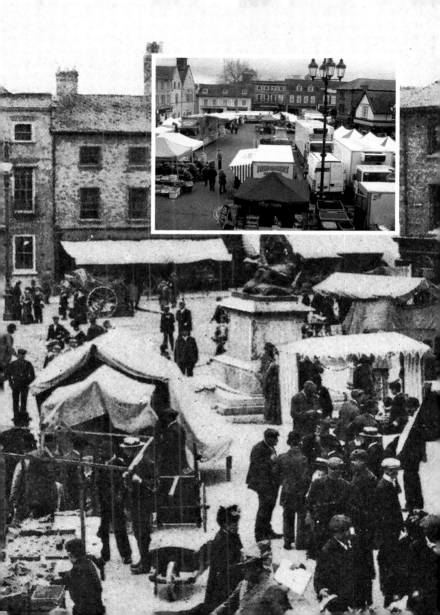

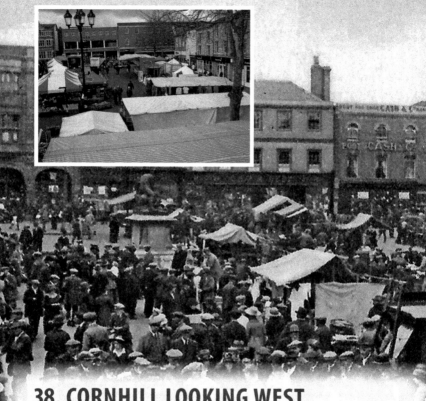

38. CORNHILL LOOKING WEST

Apart from the post office from 1895, there have been a lot of changes in this area. On the right Smiths Furnishing Co. along with the Castle Hotel have gone, the latter replaced by Superdrug. Also gone is Cash & Co, Boots stores, grocers Liptons and Maypole, Stead & Simpsons shoe shop and Woolworths. The promised link to the Arc shopping development using Market Thoroughfare alongside the post office never did materialize. The industrious market is still held twice weekly.

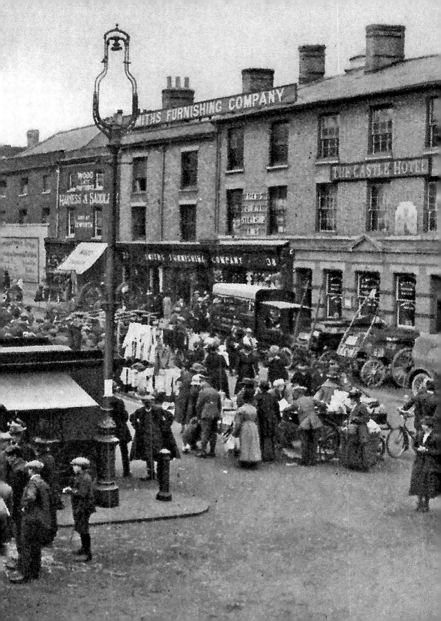

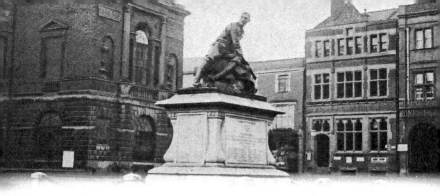

39. CORNHILL, SOUTH AFRICAN WAR MEMORIAL

Known today as The Boer War Memorial, this island monument by celebrated sculptor A. G. Walker was unveiled by Lord Methuen on the auspicious date of 11 November 1904. Then it was surrounded by volleys of rifle fire by soldiers to the 193 men from all over Suffolk who died in the conflict; they had served in various regiments. Today, it is normally surrounded by parked cars and stalls on market days, but still looking no different from yesteryear.

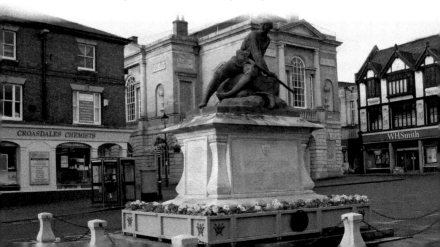

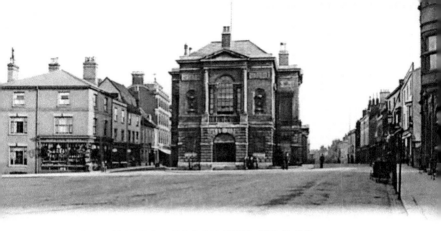

40. CORNHILL, MARKET CROSS

A public building on the Cornhill has been here for hundreds of years in one form or another. The elegant Market Cross dates from 1775/76 to designs by Robert Adam and wonderful stone carvings by local mason Thomas Singleton. The top floor, a theatre until 1819, became concert rooms with the opening of the Theatre Royal. In 1972 it became the town's art gallery, later rebranded as Smiths Row (closed 2015). The ground floor had been used for municipal purposes for many years, both functions no longer in use.

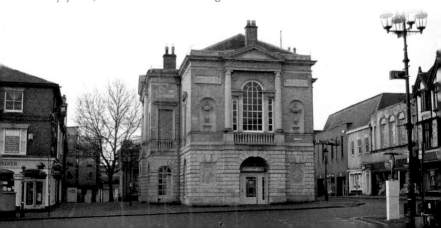

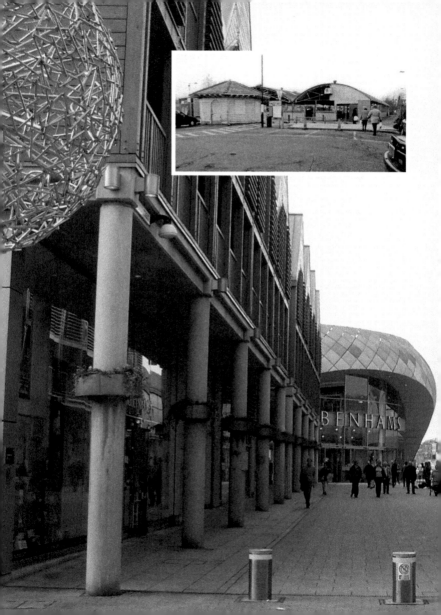

41. THE ARC, SETTLERS HUT

Often referred to as the Round House, this wooden hut has a very special place in the town's history. Built around 1864, it was used to settle accounts between buyers and sellers on market day at the cattle market. With this now gone, a battle to try and save it has started. Put into storage, Bury St Edmunds lost out mainly due to disinterest by developers, The Museum of East Anglian Life now displays it and the Arc shopping development now attracts those wanting a retail experience.

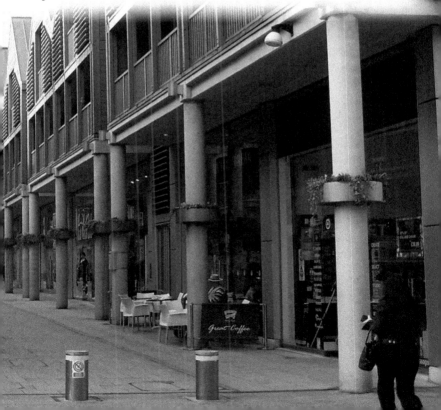

42. RISBYGATE STREET, C. J. BOWERS & SON

Charles and George's motorcycle business started at No. 98a Risbygate Street, a former stable in 1928. It soon expanded, taking over a private house and Barlow's commercial hotel at No. 100, which had just closed. An increase in sales led to further expansion by George's son Brian in 1988 when they moved over the road to Nos 11 and 13, where the Chevron fuel station used to be. 2013 saw this family-orientated business celebrate twenty-five years here on this site.

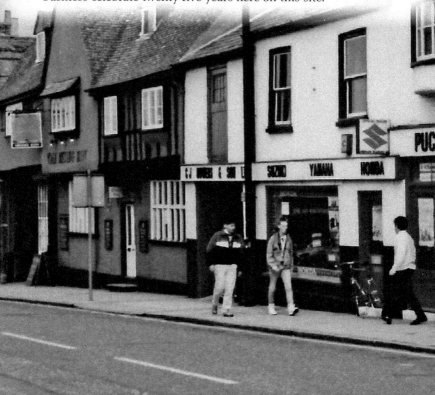

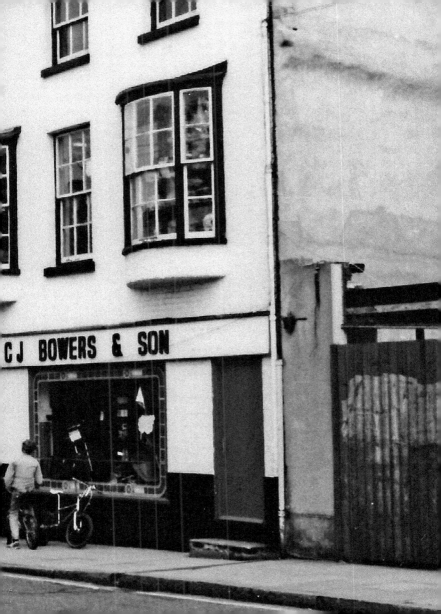

43. ST JOHNS STREET

This street showing the ancient King's Head on the left was once known as Long Brackland, but was renamed after St John's church was built in 1841/42. The street was saved from wanton destruction in 1970 by concerned residents when the planners wanted to raze it to the ground, replacing it with concrete monoliths serving as shops. Thankfully the eclectic mix of independent shops are with us today due to the vigilance of Bury residents, some of whom formed The Bury Society in 1971, a civic society still with us.

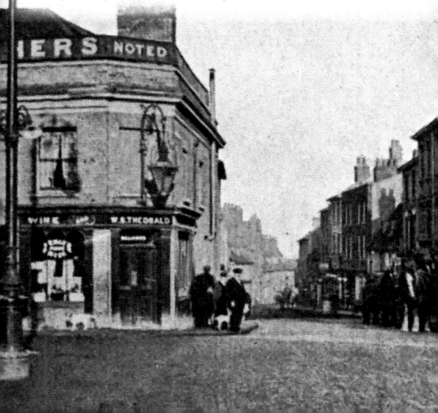

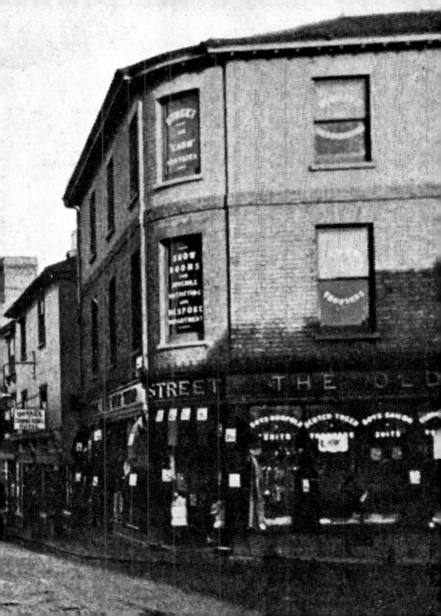

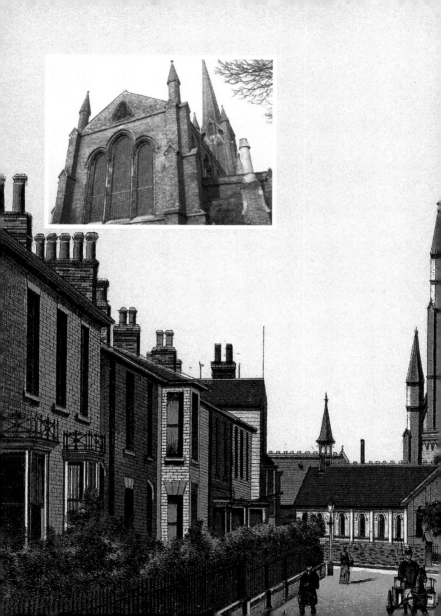

44. ST JOHN'S CHURCH

The parish church of St John the Evangelist was the first to be built in the town following the dissolution of the abbey in 1539, a much-needed addition to St Mary's and St James's. Built to designs by William Ranger, it is unusual as it is brick constructed. Consecrated in 1842, its spire has been taken at different times to be the cathedral due to its prominence on the Bury skyline. This church, along with All Saints and St Georges, is part of the same benefice.

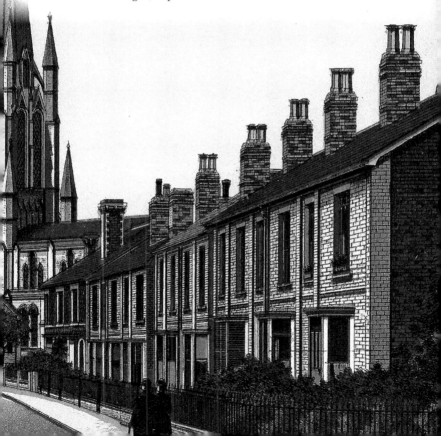

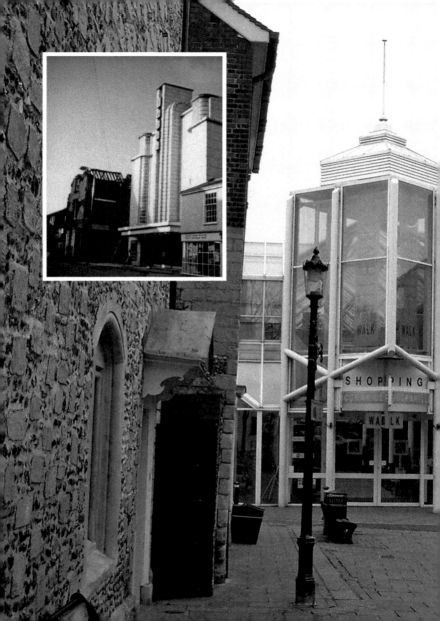

45. BRENTGOVEL STREET, CORNHILL WALK

Redevelopment of Brentgovel Street meant the demolition of the Art Deco cinema simply known as the Odeon, the Eastern Counties bus station and the eighteenth-century White Lion Inn whose yard was in great demand by carriers until the beginnings of the twentieth century. Also lost were a barber's and auctioneers; in their place was built a shopping mall. The future of this complex is very much in abeyance as the units are underused.

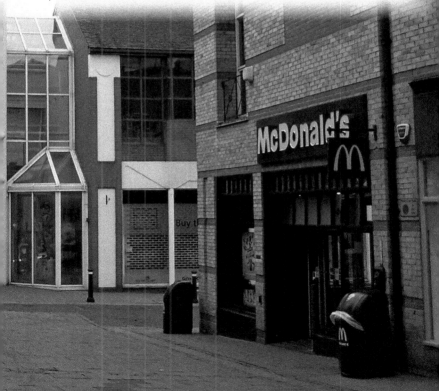

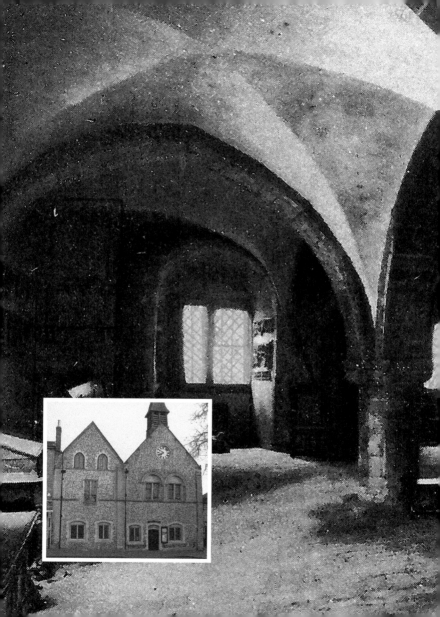

46. CORNHILL, MOYSES HALL

Once thought to be a Jewish synagogue from the late twelfth century, its proximity to a part of the market known as Hogs Hill debunks this theory. It escaped the ravages of the great fire of Bury in 1608 and went on to become a jail, left-luggage office and police station. In 1899 it became the Borough Museum, housing many eclectic collections and gruesome relics such as those of infamous murderer William Corder. In recent years much of the famous Gershom Parkington clock collection has been put on show here.

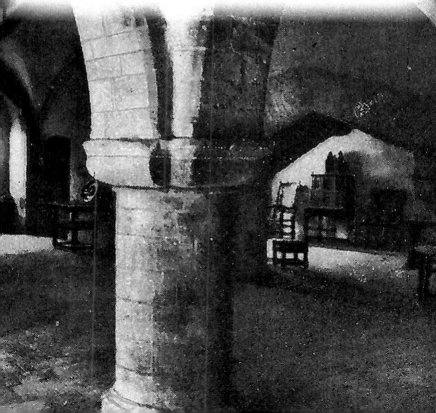

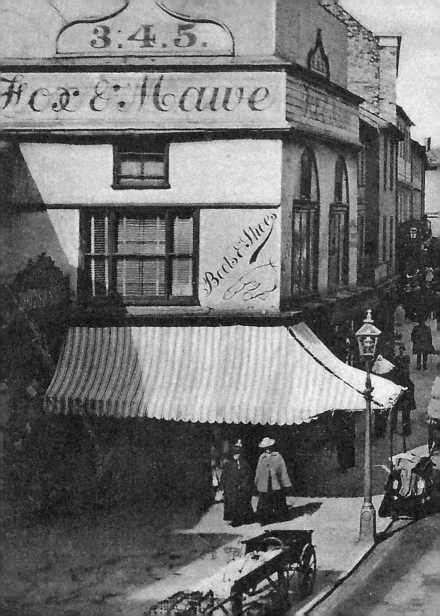

47. BUTTERMARKET

The few changes here are the buildings usage. Fox & Mawes boot & shoe shop has gone through various reincarnations including W. H. Cullen & Son, outfitters. The Suffolk Hotel on the right was once known as Le Greyhounde and was a coaching inn at one time; it closed in 1996 and was converted into two shops. In the distance is the ever-constant Moyses Hall, the Borough Museum. One major difference today is the traffic management – horse traffic was far more sedate.

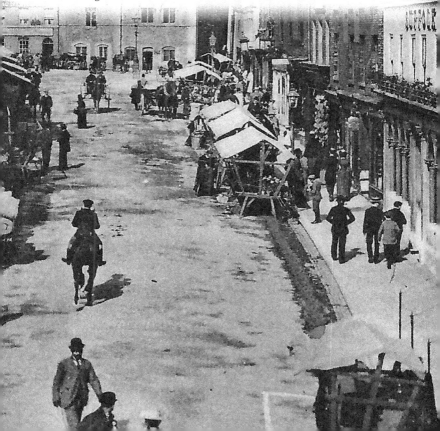

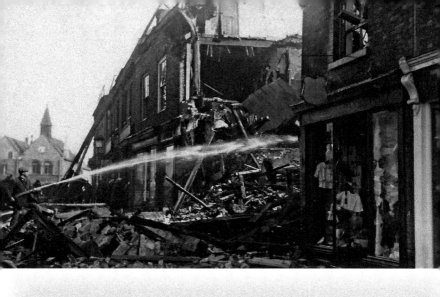

48. BUTTERMARKET, ZEPPELIN RAID

The reality of war on your doorstep was brought home to Bury residents when in 1915 a Zeppelin airship dropped its cargo of destruction on Nos 30 and 31 Buttermarket, resulting in several shops being destroyed including a bootmaker, ladies outfitters and a dyer. Thankfully there were no fatalities, but that was to change a year later when seven innocent people were to die in another aerial attack in different parts of the town.

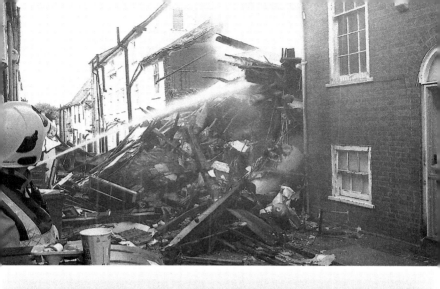

49. TRAVERSE, CUPOLA FIRE

A fine restoration in 2003 saved this iconic building of 1693 which was on the 'at risk' register. It went on to become owned by Strada, a national chain of Italian restaurants. As such a terrible fire happened in June 2012 when a fire started in the kitchen in one of the cellars. The flames spread quickly, engulfing the building. Thankfully there were no injuries. Will the restored building be a pastiche of what was once there?

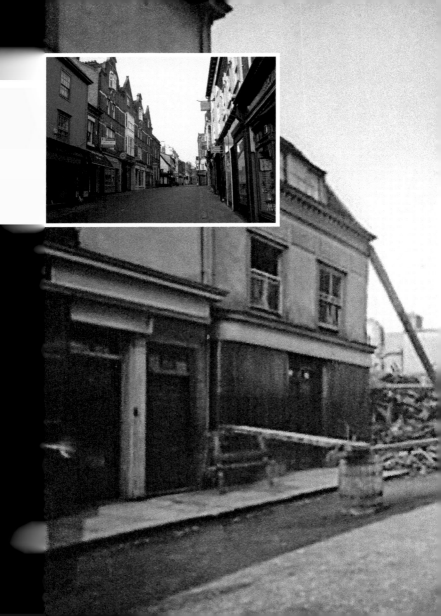

50. ABBEYGATE STREET FIRE

This is one of several amazing photographs taken by W. S. Spanton who had his photographic premises opposite this devastating fire of 1882. It had been set by failed tobacconist Simon Last whose shop was near to the Hatter Street corner. The embers were still smouldering when Last's insurance claim went in! The results of all this were five years' hard labour for him, creation of the Borough Fire Brigade and the building line being set back.

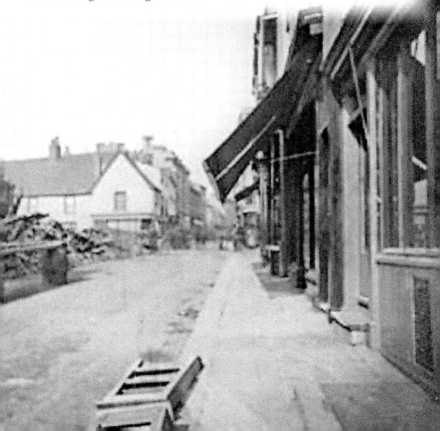

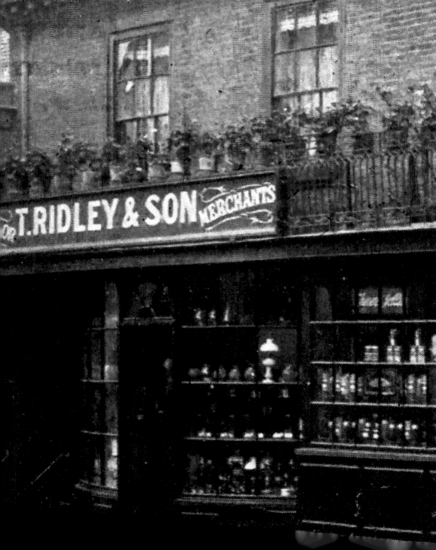

51. ABBEYGATE STREET, RIDLEY'S

This superlative grocery business run by the Ridley family at No. 36 Abbeygate Street started in 1801 in a building dating from around 1700. Thomas Ridley became twice mayor of the town in 1878 and 1882. In later years the business even went on to sell decorating materials next door. However, it was the wonderful evocative smells of cheeses, coffee beans and cured meats that met you as you crossed the threshold that many people can remember. Sadly due to rising rates it closed in 1996, being replaced by Café Uno restaurant and then Prezzo.

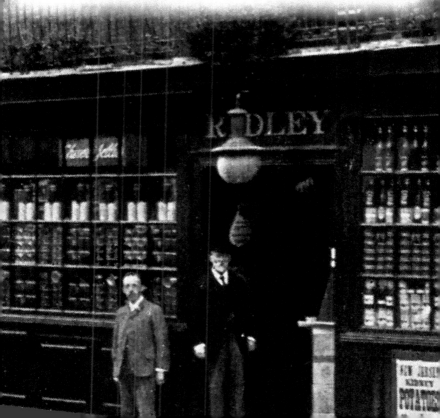

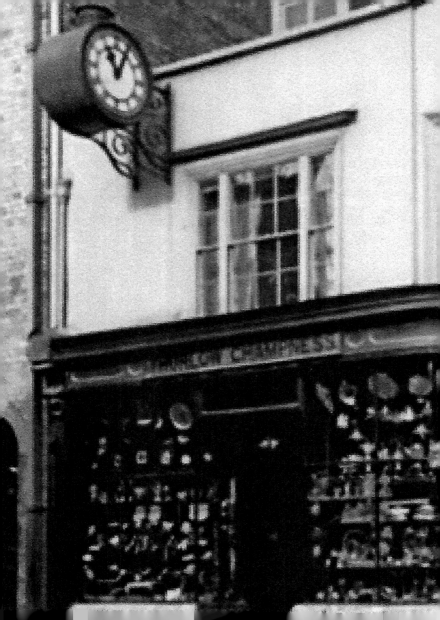

52. ABBEYGATE STREET, THURLOW CHAMPNESS

This is one of the oldest surviving businesses in the town. Its premises, No. 14 Abbeygate Street, is steeped in history with a timber-framed core going back to the sixteenth century. The entrance today is on the corner, but in Victorian times was on the front of Abbeygate Street where there is a window now. One of the shop's most striking features is the large hanging clock visible down the whole length of the street. It was made by Leeds firm Potts & Co. in 1900.

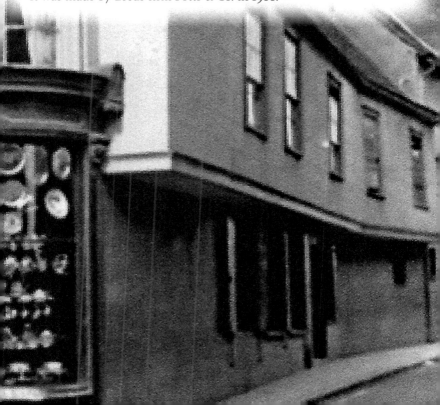

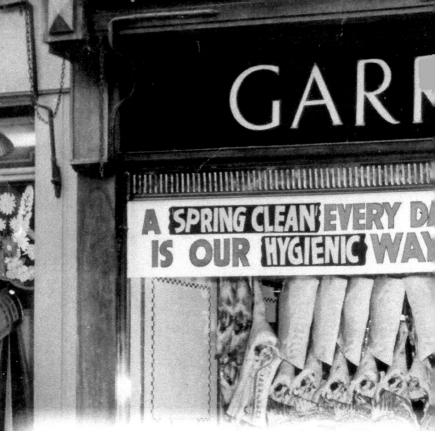

53. ABBEYGATE STREET, GARRARD'S

This butchers shop at No. 28 Abbeygate Street was one of two Garrards in the town; the other was in Out Risbygate. W. H. Garrard advertised as 'The Hygenic Butcher', gaining a reputation as butcher of high quality. Garrards finished in August 1985, being taken over by the Dewhurst chain. Eventually this closed too and became Trotter and Deane in 1991. The shop front was redesigned by Modece architects in 2012. Managing director John Deane-Bowers was at the forefront of an upmarket clothiers.

ARD'S

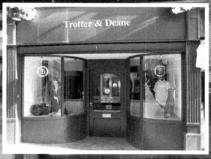

Trotter & Deane

28

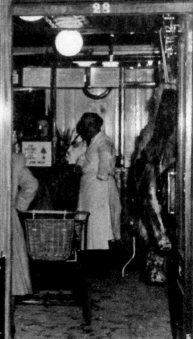

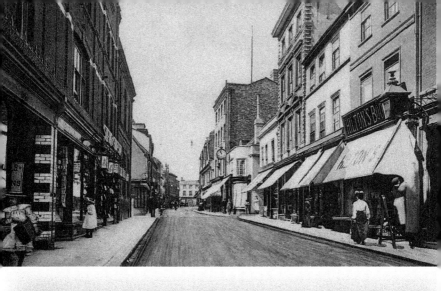

54. ABBEYGATE STREET LOOKING WEST

This is probably Bury's premier shopping street, once known as The Cook Row, the name change coming at the end of the eighteenth century when the shop fronts, no better than stalls, were enclosed. The awnings have now gone, as have the tarred wooden blocks that once made up the road. In 1882 a disastrous fire burnt down several buildings. The large number of coffee shops and restaurants have led to a so-called 'café culture'.

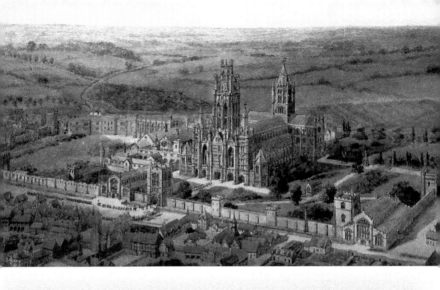

55. ST EDMUNDSBURY ABBEY CHURCH

Bury St Edmunds' very existence is because the blessed saint's body was enshrined in the huge Romanesque abbey church, part of one of the largest abbeys in the country. The length of the church meant you could get St James Cathedral and St Marys in end to end. The western tower has a lantern as at Ely cathedral, which is pure supposition on behalf of nineteenth-century artist W. K. Hardy. The picture is on show in the cathedral.

ACKNOWLEDGEMENTS

Amberley publishing are to be thanked for coming up with the idea of using a major part of my first book for them, *Bury St Edmunds Through Time*, as a guidebook. I have added several more photographs from various sources for which I am grateful. I would also like to thank the Bury St Edmunds Past & Present Society and the Suffolk Records Office who enabled me to use images from The Spanton Jarman Collection and the Dean & Chapter of St Edmundsbury Diocese for the usage of the W. Hardy interpretation of the abbey church. To those not mentioned they know who they are – thank you. Lastly but not least, thank you to my wife Sandie.